Stress Relieving Adult Book Coloring Designs

Peaceful Patterns Featuring Mandala and Mind Calming Designs With Henna Inspired Flowers

By Dorothy Mohl

You Can Check Out My Other Coloring Books & Other Books By Searching My Name (Dorothy Mohl) On Amazon. If You Liked The Book, I Would Appreciate If You Posted A Review On Amazon.

Thank You! I hope You Enjoyed!

www.ingramcontent.com/pod-product-compliance
Lightning Source LLC
Chambersburg PA
CBHW061953280526
45787CB00004B/1838